Sleeping Through
Faith Lawrence

smith|doorstop

Published 2019 by
Smith|Doorstop Books
The Poetry Business
Campo House
54 Campo Lane
Sheffield S1 2EG

Designed and Typeset by Utter
Printed by Biddles Books
Cover Image: Bax Walker Archive / Alamy Stock Photo

Smith|Doorstop Books are a member of Inpress:
www.inpressbooks.co.uk. Distributed by NBN International, Airport
Business Centre, 10 Thornbury Road Plymouth PL6 7PP

The Poetry Business gratefully acknowledges the support
of Arts Council England.

Supported by
ARTS COUNCIL
ENGLAND

Contents

For Nell

I

Grace

Of the visitors
that spring

I remember
the queen bee

levitating her heavy
body through

an open window
her balance

in resistance,
her hovering

at the very edge
of probability

Futures

September 2008

It was blue weather on the island
for both of us that day – no ghosts
on the paths, no phones.

We were listening to birds, to gulleys
talking in wind and cave-rush,
to our own small hopes.

For a while the future untethered –
whistled off into the sky like a tern,
as if it had always been provisional.

Delivery

Baby, you took your time;
nothing else was in the world
until you found that ring
of bone, and clever as a key
you turned, slipped right
through and unlocked me.

Summer Born

What sadness you will meet
I cannot tell

all I can promise
is a hole in the hedgerow

its hawthorn and heat
a floor of dry earth

foxgloves towering
with their attendant bees,

a nest shaped to both
of us, somehow.

Sleeping Through

He wakes, reaches
for my hand and says
'it's *very* morning',
which is true.
The sky is lanolin,
dressed for business
as he kisses me
and smiles with that
rough new
tenderness of his –
then it's time to get up,
time for breakfast,
and this is why
I write no poems,
my boy singing
to his tiny trains,
a day with no interstices,
beautiful as usual.

Mothers

What do the children
looking up at us
make of their mothers,

always shouting
and rewarding,
as steady and forlorn

as the limes breathing
the last of their leaves
over the garden?

Close

Now evening comes
the way you slow
down a swing –

the way you hold
your child to the seat
to steady them.

II

Flowering

after eleven paintings by Sophie Breakenridge

Birth

It doesn't matter
about the angle
of your arrival

Bloom

How heavy the present is
how difficult to carry
but the earth's still bent
on making the future –
such pockets of *colour* ...

Celandine

None of us were lonely
in the forest –
we'd no idea of sky –
when light fell through
the trees we thought
it was pollen glowing
in the earth's darkness.

Avatars

Poor flowers –
thrown into wreaths
instead of meadows;
dreaming of bees.

Macabre

Dance as though you
were protected,

as if the earth would hold you
kindly to its surface.

Home

When we were younger –
would we have settled
for this scrubland,
this tentative shelter?

Annual

The poppy blooms once
and then it's over.

But look! There are the seeds,
those emblems of pleasure.

Pod

Milk and seeds
ready for time-travel
our dark capsule.

Field

To see ourselves like this:
from a distance –
only in the deepest of dreams.

Mourning

A courtesy,
this leaning towards
the lost ones

Signal

None of us knows where
the cornfield ends

but the wind brings us
news of a flower

on the far side –
one of our own kind.

III

Three Songs

for Delia Derbyshire

Moogies Bloogis

It's a little innocent love song
for girls in mini-skirts, for knees
winking in the rain; nothing like
'I love you, I love you'
or 'you've gone, you've gone'.

I wanted something quite new
and that means discipline;
otherwise I find myself going,
'Oh I like this, I like that –
I want it, I want it all at once!'

Ziwzeh Ziwzeh Oooh Oooh Oooh

So this big boss robot
starts a new religion;
he's like the high priest
and all the other robots
sing this hymn to him.

The actors, I get them to chant,
'Praise to the master,
his wisdom and glory!';
we play it backwards,
until there's a rhythm.

I use a single note
and then do little glissandos –
but the 'Ooh-ooh-ooh'?
that isn't me at all –
that's wobbulator, pure wobbulator.

Doctor Who Theme

It's the air raid sirens
I heard as a child
not knowing where

in the universe
they came from, only
that no human music

could ever be as remote
as this. Then there's
the all-clear

bald as a star
clean as plainsong
pure as the words

they gave me to think with,
the sweep and swoop
of them falling,

like a question
or a benediction.

This sequence uses the language of Delia Derbyshire (BBC studio manager, and a pioneer of electronic music) taken from interviews in which she explores writing the pieces: 'Moogies Bloogis', 'Ziwzeh Ziwzeh Oooh Oooh Oooh', and the 'Doctor Who Theme'.

IV

Thawing

Versions after 'Le Mot Joie' by Philippe Jaccottet

Hope

February, and piles of leaves
are burning in the gardens –
it's not about clearing up,
more about kindling the light:
is it beyond us to do the same
with our diffident hearts?

In Bud

A grey day,
but here and there
new leaves
like pale flames
coursing through
the lime trees ...

Portal

Shadow of ash trees in the afternoon;
copper on snow –

then downhill to meet the clouds
to hear the river moving beneath
the mist, its stole of white fur.

Hush now! Whatever you say
will muffle the sound.
Listen: the doors are opening

Daylight

lingering on yellow stone
won't you make me whole?
Sun, you're getting braver, warmer –
can't you solder my heart?

Time now to rise, to brush the shadow
and ice from your shoulders –
my only thought is to follow you,
to have you enter me completely.

February's here again, and you're a fighter,
back on your feet, ready to win;
let me ride on your shoulders,
bathe my eyes, bring me to my senses,
tear me from this brown earth
before I fill my mouth with it
like the coward I am.

I can only talk in fragments, stones
with their own cast of shadows
on which we cannot help but fall –
splintered, scattered as we are.

V

Windfall

I watched it growing
all summer –
a little nub on the tree

outside my window,
in its ruffle of leaves,
with the lovely hard

hopefulness that belongs
to small apples until
it ripened and fell.

There was something
shameless about the way
the soil was taking it,

as if its edges meant
nothing, as if it had always
belonged to the earth.

It was all green

a mile down   and the walls
were heavy with moss and rain
and we were   falling

into a graveyard of green
until there was darkness
and then   just   the memory of green;

I thought
            this is like dying
if dying could be held   in the mind
if you could hold me
this far down

The Abduction

Now that Persephone was alone, Hades seized her
and carried her off into the Underworld.

It was the time of quiet trees,
and fruit rotting
on the forest floor.

Then your sudden grip,
our quickened breath,
my heart was a bee in a half-closed fist.

The dress my mother made was torn,
stained with grass
and asphodels.

I wear it,
walk the sunless coast
where nothing falls
but ashen rain.

Afterlife

Heaven is a lido on the coast
where the dead are playing catch
in swimming costumes
and flowery bathing caps;
everyone's losing their teeth
but they seem to be loving it.

Look at the lunches they bring:
ham sandwiches and crisps,
fruit and sponge cake for afters.
Hear them laughing on the sand,
the waves hushing their rumours
as they glide beneath the water.

Ritual

When I was locked out last night
the house was all lit up, glowing
like a church on Christmas Eve –
I saw men and women in the hallway
walking in silence, trailing
long grey robes up the staircase
and I knew they were heading
for the room where you were sleeping.
They seemed to be expecting
a birth or a death – but of that
I cannot tell you anything.

Leeds 1975

This night-day, day-night bus is the first, last,
only emissary of the lighted world,
the thin-as-care suburb of lino and candlewick.

A sigh, a stutter, a final choke.
Two slippered figures at the stop
step forward, then back.

They don't know how cold they are.

Quieting

The end of the world
when it comes, will not mean
more of everything

but less. No wind, no rain
the winter sun barely
making it over our hedge.

Gift

Dark at five. The gift of winter
is to limit us, to make morning
in an hour, the day in miniature.

Acknowledgements

An earlier version of 'Afterlife' appeared in *Poetry Review*, 'Three Songs' was
published on the BBC's Gateway website. The original Philippe Jaccottet
poems can be found in *Under Clouded Skies with Beauregard* (Bloodaxe),
with translations by David Constantine and Mark Treharne. 'Leeds 1975' was
included in the St Andrews M.Litt. anthology *Stolen Weather*.

Thanks to Peter Sansom for his care in editing this pamphlet, to Carol Ann
Duffy (especially for valuing the 'short' poem), to Eleanor Holmshaw – and to
all those who offered kind attention along the way (including Kathleen Jamie,
Douglas Dunn, Ian McMillan, Jacob Polley, Gillian Clarke, Donovan
McAbee, Sophie Breakenridge, Rachael Boast and Sue Roberts). Thanks also
to Don Paterson for his generous listening across many of these poems,
To my parents for all their support, to my Nanas – Nell and Sylvia, to Laurie
(for the unlocking and more), and to Ian – with love.

About the author

Faith Lawrence lives in Manchester and makes programmes about language and poetry for BBC Radio. She wrote about the art of listening for her Creative Writing PhD at the University of St Andrews, and is compiling a glossary of 'listening' words (whilst keeping an ear out for her young son, who is usually quite easy to hear). Her poems have been included in *Poetry Review* and *The Interpreter's House*, and she has also published critical essays on listening and poetry.

'Even as the roots of these poems go searching deep down into what 'had always / belonged to the earth', they show off such gorgeous light and lucidity. A brilliant debut.'

– Jacob Polley

'Faith Lawrence thinks about language more than anybody else I've ever met. This language-care is obvious in these poems that examine parenthood's unfathomable rules, the struggle to simply be alive in this crashing decade, and the hope that somehow poetry can be a kind of 3-D printer of, if not solutions, then possibilities.'

- Ian McMillan

smith|doorstop

ISBN 978-1-912196-65-4

9 781912 196654 >

ARTS COUNCIL ENGLAND

£7.50